When a Cat Ruled the World

Elizabeth Laird

Illustrated by
Meilo So
Galia Bernstein
Yannick Robert

CONTENTS

OXFORD
UNIVERSITY PRESS

Dear Reader,

All around the world, people keep cats. Long ago, the Ancient Egyptians thought that cats were like gods and worshipped them. In Europe, some people thought that cats were magical and had special powers.

Here are three very old stories about cats. The first is a myth about the laziness of cats. The second is about a greedy, cunning cat. The last story has a ghostly touch to it.

I hope you enjoy them all.

Elizabeth Laird

When a Cat Ruled the World

A myth from China

At the very beginning of time, the world was bright and new and shiny. But the gods had a problem.

'Who's going to be in charge?' they asked each other. 'Somebody needs to run the place, or things will go wrong.'

At that moment, a cat walked past. He looked serious and clever.

He looked as if he was thinking great thoughts. The gods looked at each other and nodded.

'That's the one,' they all said. 'He'll be a perfect leader.'

And so the cat became the ruler of the world.

The cat was clever but he was also very lazy. He didn't like working. He liked to lie in the sunshine. He liked to lick his paws and think about mice.

After a while, the gods decided to visit the world and see how it was going.

'How are things down here?' one of them asked the cat. 'Any problems? The world is running smoothly, isn't it?'

'Well, if you must know,' said the cat, 'I'm not sure. I've been busy chasing butterflies.'

'If you are the ruler of the world, you'll have to do more than chase butterflies!' another god said sternly. 'Please try harder.'

'Try harder?' yawned the cat. 'Oh yes, if you like. You can rely on me.'

But the cat didn't try harder. The cherry trees were in flower. Pink and white blossoms were falling down on to the grass. The cat was having far too much fun playing with them to think about ruling the world.

A little while later the gods came
back again.

'Why are you messing about in the cherry
blossom?' they said crossly. 'There's a world
to run! What about doing some work for
a change?'

'Work? Running the world? Oh yes, sorry,
I forgot,' said the cat. 'I'll stop playing and get
on with it. I promise.'

Off went the gods, hoping for the best.
But as soon as they had gone, the cat felt
rather tired.

'I'll just have a little nap,' he said to himself.
'I'll start ruling the world when I wake up.'

But when he woke up from his nap, he wanted to wash his ears.

Then a mouse came by and he chased it for a while.

Then he saw a dandelion clock and had fun blowing all the seeds away.

The gods came back for a third time.

'It's no good,' said the cat, before they could say a word.

'I can't rule the world. Work is just too boring! There are so many other things that I want to do. Couldn't you find someone else to look after everything?'

The gods frowned. They were angry. The cat had let them down.

Then the cat had an idea. 'I know!' he said. 'There are animals with two legs running around everywhere. They're always trying to boss the rest of us around. They poke their noses into everyone's business. Wouldn't they do?'

'Oh, you mean the people,' said the gods. 'Well, we could make them the rulers of the world. But if we do, we'll have to take something away from you and give it to them.'

'Take anything you like!' said the cat. 'I don't mind, as long as I can just please myself. Look, there's a leaf falling over there. I must go and chase it!'

And off he ran.

'You won't be able to talk anymore!' the gods shouted after him. 'We'll take away your power of speech and give it to the people!'

But the cat didn't hear. He was having too much fun playing with the falling leaves.

From that day on, no cat ever said a word. The people began to talk instead. And once the people started to talk there was no stopping them! The people worked hard looking after the world. They liked being in charge. And the cats? The cats were happy too. They had all the time in the world to play, and sleep, and chase after mice.

The gods still felt that the cats should help in some way. So, they made the cats into walking clocks. To this very day, in the early morning, you will notice that the eyes of cats are round and dark and deep.

As the sun gets higher in the sky, their eyes change into slits.

In the evening, they open out into round pools of blackness again.

There's another reason why cats are still important. When you hear them purr, you are hearing the wheels that turn the world. If the cats stopped purring, the world would stop moving. There would be no day and no night, no summer and no winter.

So now you know why cats are so smug. They know they are clever and important, but they are also free. They do whatever they want, whenever they want.

Samson and the Scaredy Cats

A folk tale from Russia

One fine day, a fox ran out of the deep, dark Russian forest. At the same time, a cat ran out of the village close by.

'Who are you?' said the fox.

'I'm Samson Cat,' said the cat. 'And who are you?'

'I'm Widow Fox,' answered the fox. 'Where do you live?'

'Nowhere, really,' said the cat. 'What about you?'

'In my cottage in the forest,' said Widow Fox. 'You can live with me there if you like.'

So Samson Cat and Widow Fox set up house together.

One day, Samson went into the forest to look for berries. He bent down to pick a nice, juicy strawberry. Just then, a hare came bounding along. The hare was in a great hurry and wasn't looking where he was going. *Bump!* He landed right on top of Samson.

'Eek! Hsss!' shrieked Samson, leaping up so
that the hare was hurled across the path.

'Aaah!' yelled the hare, as he struck the
ground with a painful thud. The world spun
around him. Then he scrambled to his feet
and raced off, as fast as the wind.

Soon, the hare met a wolf.

'What's the matter with you?' said the wolf.

'You'll never believe it,' shuddered the hare, 'but I've just escaped with my life! I was running past Widow Fox's cottage, when a huge beast leaped out from nowhere. It tried to kill me, but I put up a great fight and managed to run away.'

'You don't say!' said the wolf. 'I'd better go
and have a look myself.'

'Take care,' said the hare. 'This monster is
so big and scary that ...'

But he was talking to the air. The wolf had
already run off towards Widow Fox's cottage.

Now that morning, Widow Fox had caught a fat lamb. She and Samson were in the kitchen, gobbling it up for their lunch. The wolf paused outside the garden gate and coughed politely. Widow Fox went to see who was there. She wasn't at all pleased to see the wolf.

'I don't want him to see our lunch,' she thought. 'If he does, he'll take it away and have it for himself.'

But she smiled politely, all the same.

'Who's that in your kitchen, Widow Fox?' asked the wolf. 'I can hear bones crunching. I can hear jaws grinding. I can hear lips smacking. It's making me feel quite hungry.'

'Ooh,' said Widow Fox, pretending to look scared. 'That's Samson Cat. He killed a huge ram in a fight, and now he's eating it up. He's always so hungry. You'd better run away, or he'll do the same to you.'

The wolf cocked his head and listened. All he could hear was *Chomp! Scrunch! Chomp! Munch!* coming from the cottage. But he thought the cat was saying 'Not enough! Not enough!'

If a whole sheep's not enough for him, he thought, he'll be after me next. His fur stood on end with fright.

'I'm out of here!' he shouted, and away he ran.

Munch!

Scrunch!

Chomp!

After a while, he met a badger, who was rooting round in the earth looking for worms.

'I wouldn't stay around these parts, if I were you,' the wolf said to the badger. 'There's a scary new monster in this forest. He eats four sheep every day, and he's still hungry after that!'

'Eh?' snuffled the badger. He lifted his black nose in the air and stretched his claws. 'A monster? I'd like to see him for myself.'

'Don't be a fool,' said the wolf. 'He's particularly fond of badgers. He'll have you for his tea.'

While they were talking, a bear came by.

'Have you heard the news?' called out the badger. 'There's a monster living in Widow Fox's cottage. He eats ten cows a day, and he's still hungry after that.'

'Ten cows a day?' said the bear. 'I'd like to see that. Perhaps Widow Fox would let us have a peep at him, if we ask her ever so nicely?'

'Well – maybe, but I don't dare,' said the wolf.

'I don't either,' said the bear.

They both looked at the badger.

'All right,' he said, trying to look brave. 'I'll go and talk to Widow Fox.'

So the badger scurried off to Widow Fox's cottage.

He was so scared that his little heart beat
fast inside his chest. He tiptoed up to the
door, and knocked politely. The wolf and
the bear were peering over the fence,
watching him.

'S-sorry to b-bother you, Widow Fox,' stammered the badger, when Widow Fox opened the door. 'But my friends and I have heard of the monst – I mean, the animal who is living with you. We would like to see him, but we don't want to get eaten up.'

Widow Fox hid a smile, and pretended to think.

'Well,' she said at last, 'why don't you invite us to visit you? You'll have to bake *mountains* of pies, and fetch in jars and *jars* full of honey. But if you give him all that to eat, perhaps he won't eat *you*.'

The three friends ran off, and began to get ready.

The wolf baked dozens of pies.

The bear brought back buckets full of honey from the forest.

And the badger cleaned his lair from top to bottom.

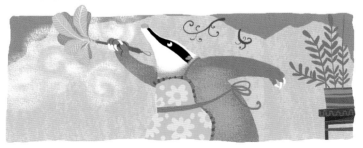

When everything was ready, the three of them were hot and tired.

'I need a rest,' yawned the wolf.

He found a big log and lay down beside it for a little snooze.

'I could sleep for a week,' said the badger.

He staggered to a bush and crawled underneath, where it was cool.

'I'll climb up a tree,' said the bear, 'and keep watch. I'll let you know when they're coming.'

But his eyes were closing, and soon he was snoring, just like the other two.

Not long after, along came Widow Fox and Samson Cat. They pushed the door open and went inside the badger's lair.

'Where is everyone?' said Widow Fox.

'I don't know,' said Samson, 'but look at all those pies!'

'And look at all that honey!' said Widow Fox.

Without saying another word, they began to stuff themselves.

Outside, under his bush, the badger had woken up. He could hear noises coming from inside his lair.

Chomp! Munch! Chomp! Scrunch!

'Not enough!' he thought. 'It's the monster, and he's saying "Not enough!"'

Terrified, he tried to wriggle further under the bush. Soon, only the tip of his fluffy black tail was showing.

At that moment, Samson looked out of the window. He saw something black and furry twitching near the bush.

'A mouse!' he thought. 'I'll soon have *him*.'

He jumped out of the window, and grabbed hold of the badger's tail.

The badger yelped and scrambled away. But he was in such a panic he didn't look where he was going. He crashed straight into the bear's tree. He shook it so hard that the bear fell out and landed on top of the wolf.

'The monster! The monster!' yelled the
wolf. He leaped up and began to run away
after his two friends.

At last, when they were quite out of breath,
they stopped running.

'Did you see how he caught hold of my tail and threw me against the tree?' said
the badger.

'Yes, and how he tore my tree out by its roots and shook it in his great big teeth?' said the bear.

'And then he beat me with the tree, so that I'm bruised all over?' said the wolf.

'Now that's what I call a monster!' said the badger, shaking his head.

'Yes, a really scary one!' said the bear.

'So now we know,' said the wolf. 'Samson Cat is the scariest monster in the whole
wide world!'

King of the Cats

A folk tale from Britain

In the old, old days of long-ago Britain, people were a little bit afraid of cats. They thought that cats had strange powers.

'You want to be careful around cats,' they would say. 'They know a bit too much about death, and the underworld, and things that might happen in the future.'

Here's one of the stories they liked to tell.

* * *

One dark night, an old woman sat beside her fire. Tom, her cat, sat beside her. His green eyes were closed.

It was a stormy night. The wind was howling round the house. It was making the windows rattle.

'Are you asleep, Tom?' asked the old woman. But the cat didn't move a whisker.

The old woman's husband, Peter the gravedigger, was out in the churchyard. Suddenly, he ran into the cottage. His hair was standing on end, and his eyes were round with fear.

'What's the matter with you?' said his wife.

'I was digging a grave,' said Peter. 'But I was so tired, I think my mind started playing tricks on me. Suddenly, I heard a cat say, *Miaow!*'

'Miaow!' echoed Tom from his corner.

'Well,' the gravedigger went on. 'I looked up, and I saw such a sight!'

He stopped, and wiped his head with his handkerchief.

'What sight?' said his wife impatiently. 'What are you talking about?'

'It was a procession of cats,' said the gravedigger. 'Nine of them there were, all black, like Tom here. And they were carrying a little coffin. And all the time they were saying, *Miaow!*'

'Miaow!' said Tom again.

'And on the coffin was a red velvet cushion, with a tiny crown of gold sitting on it. Why, look at our Tom! He's staring at me with great big eyes. Do you think he understands what I'm saying?'

'Oh, you silly man,' said his wife. 'Go on with your silly story.'

'Well, the cats were all crying out together, *Miaow! Miaow!* –'

'Miaow!' sang out Tom.

'Yes, just like that. Then one of them came right up to me and he said ...'

'What do you mean, he *said*?' said his wife. 'Cats can't speak!'

'Well, this one could,' said Peter. 'He said, "Go and tell Tom Tildrum that Tim Toldrum's dead."'

'What nonsense!' his wife said. 'I don't believe a word of it. I think you'd better get yourself to bed for an early night.'

But the gravedigger didn't move. He was staring at their cat.

Tom was growing in front of their eyes.

He was swelling up like a balloon, and his great green eyes were shining like lamps. He jumped to his four black feet, and lashed his long black tail. Then he cried out, 'Tim Toldrum's dead, is he? Then I'm the King of the Cats!'

Then, to their astonishment, Tom leaped over the fire and ran up the chimney. And that was the last the gravedigger and his wife ever saw of him.